VIKINGS
IN 30 SECONDS

PHILIP STEELE

ILLUSTRATED BY STEF MURPHY
CONSULTANT: DR. RAGNHILD LJOSLAND

IVY KIDS

Contents

About this book
. . . in 60 seconds

About 1,200 years ago, many families along the coasts of northern Europe lived in fear. They stared out to the horizon, looking for the sails of unknown ships. Rumours spread like wildfire. People said that these ships carried armed raiders who attacked towns and villages and burned down churches. They were stealing treasure and murdering people or carrying them off to become slaves.

The raiders came from Scandinavia, the region of northern Europe now made up of Denmark, Sweden and Norway. People called them Northmen and many other names. Today we generally call them Vikings. Soon these Vikings were attacking many other European countries.

The Vikings are often remembered as fierce warriors, with scary names like Eirik Bloodaxe, Thorfinn Skullsplitter or Ragnar Hairy Breeches. But, they should also be remembered because they were great traders, seafarers and explorers. They were farmers, blacksmiths, jewellers and skilled carvers of wood, stone and walrus tusk. They were poets, storytellers and law-makers.

Archaeologists have discovered hoards of Viking treasure. They have excavated a magnificent ship that was used as the tomb of a noblewoman, who was wearing a fine red dress. They have uncovered entire towns, farm buildings, forts and ports. Even rubbish pits and toilets can tell us a lot about how people used to live in the Viking age.

It's time to meet the Vikings. Every topic in this book has a page to read as fast or as slow as you like. If you are in a real hurry you can read the 3-second sum-up instead. Each full-page illustration supplies a colourful at-a-glance guide, too. Then, if you have a spare few minutes, there are extra facts to discover and exciting hands-on activities to try.

Lands and peoples

The Vikings lived in northern Europe during the Middle Ages from around 790 to 1050 CE. The Vikings developed from bands of raiders to become a powerful force in Europe. They were also great explorers, always looking to find new places to live. In about 800 CE, when their sea raids were beginning to spread fear, the map of Europe looked very different from today. Much of France, Germany and Italy was ruled by an emperor called Charlemagne, who belonged to the Frankish people. Greece and areas of southeastern Europe were part of the Byzantine empire. Britain and Ireland were made up of small kingdoms ruled by the Welsh, Scots, Picts, Anglo-Saxons and Irish.

Lands and peoples
Glossary

amber A brown, yellow or orange fossil, which is used in making jewellery.

Arctic Circle The ocean and lands that surround the North Pole and where there is midnight sun at midsummer.

assembly A public meeting or gathering.

bog iron An impure form of the metal that occurs naturally in the iron-rich water of some marshes and swamps.

Byzantine empire Lands ruled from the ancient city of Byzantium, which became Constantinople (and is now called Istanbul). It was originally the eastern part of the Roman empire.

feud A long-lasting quarrel between two people or two families.

fjord (say 'fiord') A deep-sea inlet in the coast, long and narrow with steep sides.

Frankish Of the Franks, a people living in France during the early Middle Ages. They gave their name to the country.

glacier A river of thick, very slow-moving ice.

jarl A rich and powerful nobleman, who was a member of the top class in Viking society.

karl A free male citizen in Viking society, able to own property and trade.

Middle Ages/medieval The period of European history that separates the time of ancient Rome from the modern world of discovery and science. Some historians date it from 476 CE to 1453.

Old Norse The language spoken by the Vikings.

ore Rock containing useful minerals, such as iron or gold.

outlaw Someone condemned at a trial to be cast out from society and refused the protection of the law.

pagan Someone who follows a pre-Christian or non-Christian faith.

rune One of the stick-like letters used in Viking alphabets.

saami A people also known as Lapps. They live in the north of Norway, Sweden, Finland and Russia.

thrall A Viking slave.

Homeland

... in 30 seconds

The Vikings originally came from Scandinavia – a region of mountains, forests, lakes and bogs in northern Europe. Its long coastline is broken up by deep inlets, headlands and islands. Some Vikings lived near the coasts, where there were harbours for ships and plentiful fish. Others lived in the flat lands of the south where crops could be grown.

The Vikings made their homes in scattered settlements and villages. Later, they built towns and forts. They mostly lived by farming and trading. Scandinavia could offer plenty of timber, furs and minerals such as bog iron, a useful metal ore that could easily be collected from wetlands. Amber, a yellow or brown fossil resin, was valued for making jewellery.

Although Scandinavia was a good place to live, the Vikings wanted more land. Many wanted to get rich, by trading overseas or by attacking and looting distant lands. Some wanted to find better farmland where they could build new homes, or win power and fame. Above all, Vikings were adventurers. They loved sailing off to explore and settle new lands such as Iceland and Greenland.

3-second sum-up

The Vikings came from Scandinavia, where they lived by fishing, farming and trading.

Timeline

Vendel Period (about 550–790s CE): This is the time before the Viking age, and all Viking customs and trading have their roots in this period. It takes its name from a place in Sweden.

Viking age (790s–960 CE): These years mark the high point of the Viking way of life. It was a time of overseas raiding and settlement, long-distance exploration and trade.

Christian nations (about 960–1100 CE): During this time, Christianity gradually spreads through the Viking lands and larger, more powerful kingdoms grow up.

The Vikings lived in Scandinavia, which is a partly mountainous region of northern Europe.

N
W
S

Winters in the north were dark and bitterly cold and people needed wood for fires to keep warm.

Lakes and forests provided fish and timber.

Most of the Viking population lived in the southern regions of Scandinavia where it was warmer and along the coasts where they could easily sail.

Southern farmland had warm summers but snowy winters.

Who were the Vikings?

... in 30 seconds

'Vikings' is the name we give to people living in Scandinavia between about 1,200 and 900 years ago. They were the ancestors of today's Danes, Swedes, Norwegians and Icelanders. The Vikings were related to other peoples living to the south, in Germany, and to the Anglo-Saxons who had settled in England. Some non-Viking peoples, who were ancestors of today's Saami, lived in Scandinavia, too.

At the time the Vikings were known as 'Northmen' or 'Danes', or sometimes these raiders from the sea were called pirates, pagans (non-Christians) or foreigners. All Vikings shared a similar background and way of life, but there were probably local differences in their customs or what they wore.

Although they spoke in different ways, too, they all used the same language called Old Norse. Over the centuries, as Vikings invaded and settled in other parts of Europe, Old Norse developed into some of the languages spoken in northern Europe today.

The Vikings wrote words down using letters called runes. However, at the end of the Viking age, Norse began to be written in the Roman alphabet used in other parts of western Europe.

3-second sum-up

The Vikings spoke a language called Old Norse and wrote with letters called runes.

3-minute mission Crack the code!

The Viking alphabet is called the futhark, which is the sound of its first six runes. Only 16 runes were used during Viking times.

ᚠᚢᚦᚭᚱᚴ ᚼᚾᛁᛅᛋ ᛏᛒᛦᛚ ᛌ

f u t h a r k   h n i a s   t b m l R

Can you translate these runes into modern English?

ᚦᛁᛋ ᚠᛁᛋᚭ ᛁᛋ ᚭ ᛋᚭᚭᚱᚠ
ᚦᚭᛏ ᛁᛋ ᛁᛏᛋ ᚠᛁᚾ

See page 96 for answers.

The name 'Viking' may once have been linked to a part of the Norwegian coast known as Viken, but it soon became used to describe a pirate way of life.

Vikings often attacked other people to get more land or steal possessions. The word 'Vikingr' meant going off on a voyage or raid. 'Vikingar' (Vikings) could refer to those people taking part in a raid.

Vikings carved letters called runes to tell people important messages.

All Vikings shared a similar way of life and were great craftsmen and warriors.

Society

... in 30 seconds

Viking society was divided up into different groups or classes. At the top was the king. The first Viking kings were not grand rulers living in palaces though. They often controlled quite small regions. Their power depended on their wealth, their success in war and keeping order, and support from their followers. Towards the end of the Viking age, kings became more powerful and ruled over whole countries.

Viking noblemen came next and were called jarls (earls). They were rich and powerful owners of large areas of land, horses and ships. They were expected to send warriors to support the king in battle.

Most Vikings were called karls, meaning freemen. Some were wealthy and owned land and houses, while others were poor. Karls might work as farmers, skilled craft workers, blacksmiths, shipbuilders or merchants. Most of the warriors, seafarers and settlers were karls.

At the bottom were thralls (slaves) who were forced to work very hard as labourers or servants and had few rights. Many slaves were captured during sea raids. Only a few were lucky enough to win or buy their freedom.

3-second sum-up

Viking kingdoms were divided into three main classes – nobles (jarls), freemen (karls) and slaves (thralls).

Women's world

Men ruled, but women were respected and had some rights. They needed to be tough and practical. It was the women who ran farms and homes while the men were away fighting. Women controlled the household budget and carried the keys to buildings and stores. Women were skilled spinners and weavers. They played an important part as pioneers settling new lands.

There was a strict order of society (hierarchy),
with the king at the top and
slaves at the bottom.

The king was expected to
be brave – and generous
to his followers in return
for their loyalty.

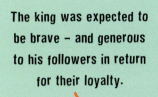

Jarls were powerful
chieftains, who might
organize raids or
trading expeditions,
and command
many warriors.

Karls were free
citizens, with the
right to own land and
trade. Most karls
were farmers.

Thralls were slaves who
had to work very hard for
their masters.

Law and order

... in 30 seconds

The Vikings had a strong sense of honour and they could be easily offended. Insults or crimes often ended in revenge and fighting, or in quarrels between families or individuals. These feuds could go on for many years.

Such problems might need to be sorted out at a public assembly, known as the Thing. Assemblies could settle arguments about property, marriage and divorce. They could question witnesses about cases of murder, injury or robbery. They could pass sentences, make new laws or even proclaim someone king.

Each assembly covered a district or a region and was held at a particular time of the year. Assemblies were gatherings of free men only. Women and slaves could not take part in the assembly, but the interests of some women could be represented. The arrangements varied from one Viking land to another. In Iceland, people met at a place called the Assembly Plain, and gathered by the Law Rock. There, a council of chieftains was held to appoint a legal expert or 'lawspeaker'.

Assemblies could not carry out the sentences they passed, as there was nothing like a police force. It was up to the victims of crime and the public to make sure that the law was enforced.

3-second sum-up

Public assemblies were held to pass laws and judge crimes.

Ancient parliaments

Viking assemblies were an early form of parliament. Some of them still exist today. The Tynwald is a parliament on the Isle of Man, one of the British Isles that was settled by the Vikings. It has been meeting for over a thousand years. The Althing is the parliament of Iceland and has been passing laws since it was founded in 930 CE, apart from a gap in the 1800s when it was abolished, then reinstated.

Arguments and problems were sorted out at a public assembly known as the Thing.

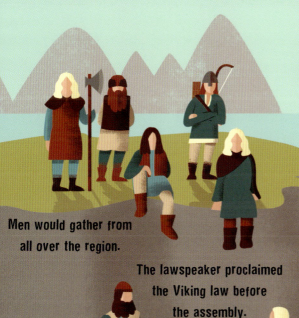

Men would gather from all over the region.

A thief might have to pay money back to his victim, as compensation.

The lawspeaker proclaimed the Viking law before the assembly.

A criminal could be exiled to a foreign land, or be declared an outlaw from society, with no rights.

Some disputes were settled by a 'holmgang', which was armed combat between two people.

Seafarers

Many Vikings lived on coasts and islands, or beside rivers. Ships were often the quickest way to travel. People in Scandinavia had been building boats for a thousand years or more, and the Vikings were the best seafarers in Europe. The sea was their route to fame and fortune, and enabled them to raid and settle in unknown lands. Viking poets loved to write about the ocean. They thought up all sorts of clever names for it – such as the 'whale-house', the 'smooth path of ships' and the 'slopes of the sea-king'.

Seafarers
Glossary

awning A wide length of cloth used for shade or shelter.

barter To trade without money, by exchanging goods or services.

bazaar A busy market, generally under a roof, in the cities of western or southern Asia.

cargo Goods being carried by a ship.

clinker-built Having a hull made of overlapping planks.

cross-beam A ship's timber that joins and strengthens the two sides of the hull.

faering A small boat used for fishing or ferrying.

haggle To bargain over a trade deal.

helmsman The sailor who steers a ship.

hull The main body of a ship, its bottom and sides.

jetty A pier or quay where boats can be tied up.

karl A free male citizen in Viking society, able to own property and trade.

keel A wooden beam running along a ship's bottom and supporting the hull.

knarr A broad Viking ship designed to carry a lot of cargo.

longphort A Viking camp or base in Ireland.

longship A long and narrow Viking ship, used in raiding and exploration.

mint To make new coins, or the place where the coins are made.

monastery The buildings of a religious community, where monks live and worship.

navigate To plan a journey, following a course.

pagan Someone who follows a pre-Christian or non-Christian faith.

plunder To loot or steal goods using force; also the term for the goods obtained by looting and violence.

prow The projecting front part of a ship.

rib A strip of wood designed to strengthen the hull of a boat.

rivet A metal fastener or bolt, which holds together two wooden timbers or metal sections.

seafarer Someone who often travels by sea, such as a sailor.

starboard As you face forwards, the right-hand side of a ship. (The left-hand side is known as the port side.)

stem The curved timber at the front of a ship that brings together the two sides of the hull.

stern The back end of a ship or boat.

strakes The planks of a ship's hull.

weather vane A flat piece of metal that moves to show the direction of the wind.

Making boats

... in 30 seconds

Building a Viking ship was very hard work. First, woodcutters chopped down trees in the forest. They stripped the trunks of their branches and then hauled them to a river bank or seashore. The best wood of all was oak, but ash, beech or pine were useful, too.

Skilled carpenters cut and shaped the timbers with axes and scrapers. Some built the hull, using iron nails and rivets. Wool or animal hair soaked in tar was stuffed between the ship's planks, known as strakes, to keep them watertight.

Viking ships were powered by oars and sails. The rowers sat on wooden chests or on benches. The biggest ships had very long oars, and a broad steering oar or rudder lashed to the starboard side, towards the stern.

Large rectangular sails were generally made of woollen cloth. This was soaked in animal grease and perhaps criss-crossed with strips of leather so that it could stand up to wind, rain or spray from the sea. Sails could be coloured or striped. Ropes made from twisted sealskin, horsehair or plant fibres supported the mast and sails.

3-second sum-up

The Vikings built first-rate rowing boats and sailing ships.

Ship shapes

Small rowing boats called faerings might be used for a day's fishing. The knarr was a big ship, with some decking ore (front) and aft (back). It was broad and deep enough to hold cargo, horses or cattle. It could be used for trading or settlement of new lands. The finest ship of all was the langskip or longship. It was slim and streamlined, ideal for long-distance raiding.

Axes are used to make wedge-shaped cuts in tree trunks.

These wedges will become the ship's strakes (planks).

The backbone of the ship is a long timber beam called the keel. It supports the hull.

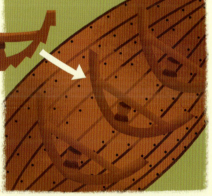

The inside of the hull is strengthened with ribs and cross-beams.

The curved stem is at the front of the keel. It joins together the two sides of the hull.

Viking ships were made very skillfully. They were clinker-built, which means that the planks of the hull overlapped each other.

The prow is tall and curved. Sometimes the wood is decorated with carvings.

The longship

... in 30 seconds

Just how long was a Viking longship? A typical vessel measured about 17 m (56 ft) and had 16 or 18 oars on either side, with one man to each oar. Some of the later warships were much bigger, needing a crew of about 80 men. The keel of a warship found at Roskilde, in Denmark, was 32 m (105 ft). It dated from about 1025 CE.

The longship was designed for the open ocean. Its timbers were strong, but they could bend slightly with the motion of the waves. The hull was narrow and streamlined. Typical speeds ranged from about 5 to 10 knots (9 to 19 km/h). The top speed would have been over 15 knots (28 km/h).

Longships were light and were also designed for use in shallow water and rivers. This made it easy for raiders to jump ashore or haul the ship onto a beach.

Longships were perfect for raiding, but did not have enough space to carry much extra cargo. They were not heavy enough to ram other ships, either. For a sea battle, several ships had to be lashed together to provide a fighting platform. Shields were sometimes slotted along the side of the ship for display or protection.

3-second sum-up

Longships were long, narrow and light. They were good in shallow waters as well as out at sea.

3-minute mission Design a longship prow

The Vikings were great woodcarvers, and they liked to decorate their best ships. Sometimes the prow of a longship was carved in the shape of a beast, a snake or a dragon. Its snarling jaws may have been intended to terrify the enemy or drive away evil spirits, or just impress other Vikings! You can design your own scary beast for a prow. Draw an outline on light card and cut it out. Draw in the detail.

A longship can be powered by sail or oars. The crew must be ready for storms, rough seas or enemy attacks.

The mast could be unstepped (taken down) if necessary.

The helmsman steered the ship using his broad steering oar as a kind of rudder.

The carved dragon prow was designed to scare the enemy or evil spirits.

Oars might be about 5–8 m (16–26 ft) long.

Decking was loose. It could be easily raised if the ship took on water and needed bailing out.

On a voyage

... in 30 seconds

Longships were open boats, with no cabins. This meant that on a voyage the crew had to put up with salty sea spray, icy winds or burning hot sun, during hour after hour of hard rowing. A large cloth or awning could be put up to shelter the rowers. This could be taken ashore, along with tents, to set up a camp.

Personal weapons, cloaks and food could be kept dry in the crew's sea chests. Dried or salted meat and fish, apples, nuts and cheese were all easily stored foods that could last through a voyage. Fresh fish could be caught on the way, and shore visits could be used for hunting or taking on fresh water.

Viking crews had no proper maps. They often followed coastlines, looking out for familiar features such as headlands. At sea, they could check currents or movements of birds. They also looked at the positions of the sun and stars. Raiding in summer months avoided darkness and winter storms.

Although longships were well built, they could still get caught by gales and giant waves so shipwrecks were common.

3-second sum-up

Longships were open to the weather and the rowing was hard. The Vikings navigated by the Sun and stars.

3-minute mission Make a wind vane

You need: • Stiff cardboard • Scissors • Gold acrylic paint • Paintbrush • Black felt-tip pen • A wooden stick • Tape
1. Draw a right angle on the cardboard, with the horizontal line measuring 10 cm (4 in) and the vertical one 6 cm (2.5 in).
2. Draw a curved shape from one line end to the other (see drawing above). Cut out the curved shape and paint it gold.
3. When it's dry, use a felt-tip pen to draw on snakes, lions, dragons or birds. Then you can tape the short side to a stick and push it loosely into the ground. Watch the wind blow it round!

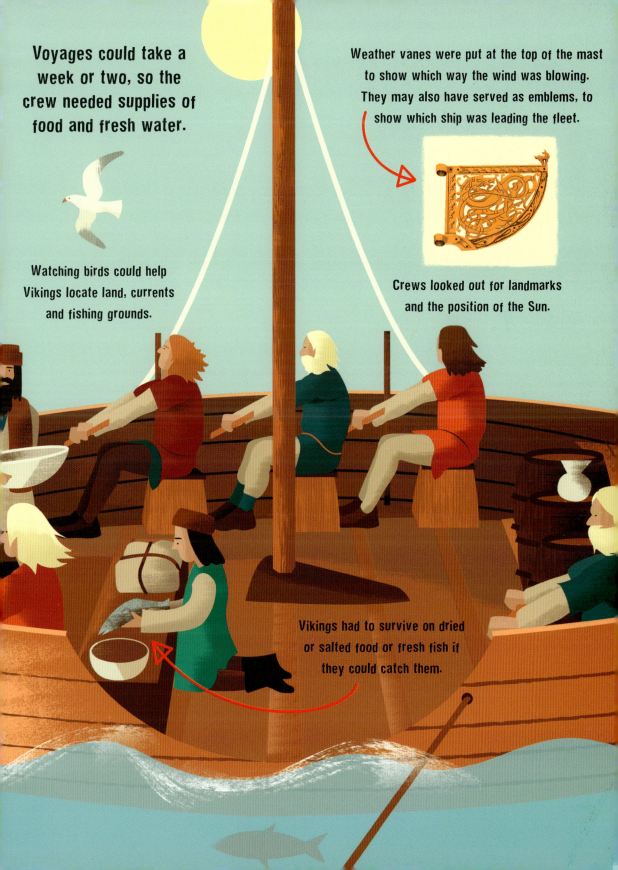

Voyages could take a week or two, so the crew needed supplies of food and fresh water.

Weather vanes were put at the top of the mast to show which way the wind was blowing. They may also have served as emblems, to show which ship was leading the fleet.

Watching birds could help Vikings locate land, currents and fishing grounds.

Crews looked out for landmarks and the position of the Sun.

Vikings had to survive on dried or salted food or fresh fish if they could catch them.

Ports and traders

... in 30 seconds

Viking merchants sailed around northern coasts, selling and buying goods, in knarrs, which were wide, deep ships with room for cargo. Viking ports such as Hedeby, in what is now Germany, had jetties where merchant ships could tie up. Viking traders sailed or rowed up rivers, too. If necessary they used smaller boats, which were light enough to be carried overland, to avoid bends in the river or rapids.

These trading expeditions were set up by groups of karls. Most of those who went could farm, row, sail or fight as well as haggle for the best deal. The Vikings traded over a large area of the world, from the icy shores of Greenland, famous for its walrus ivory, to the bazaars of Southwest Asia. They exchanged goods with many different peoples, such as Slavs, German and Baltic peoples, Franks, Anglo-Saxons, Greeks and Arabs.

Goods could be bartered (exchanged) or paid for with bars of silver. Foreign coins were soon being used, too. They were sometimes cut into pieces and valued just by the weight of their silver. In the 900s CE, as Viking kings became more powerful, they began to make some of their own coins.

3-second sum-up

Ships allowed the Vikings to trade with many different peoples and over great distances.

3-minute mission Mint some money

You need: • Silver card • Scissors • Thin-tipped black marker pen

Imagine you are a Viking king. You want to design and mint (make) some coins to show how powerful you are. The design might show a ship, an axe or a sword. Cut out some coin-sized discs from silver card, and draw on your designs with the marker pen.

The Vikings traded locally as well as in distant lands.
They bartered for goods such as amber, wine and tin
or paid with silver bars and coins.

Scandinavia and Russia were centres of the fur trade.

Germany provided swords of the finest quailty.

Silks and spices were imported from Asia.

Goods were bartered, or exchanged, with other items.

Vikings sold fish, sulphur for fire-based weapons and falcons for hunting.

Raids and plunder

... in 30 seconds

The Vikings used their fast longships to attack villages and towns along coasts and rivers. Today, we have lots of technology to warn us of an enemy attack. In the Viking age, however, villagers scarcely had time to race from the fields back to their homes before the longships were beached and armed warriors were swarming ashore.

Viking raids were brief and brutal and the attackers could make a quick getaway using their boats. The local people were murdered or captured as slaves. Buildings were burnt down. Cattle were stolen and grain stores were ransacked for food. The best plunder was items that were easy to carry – gold and silver, weapons, tools, clothes, furs and jewellery.

The Vikings often targeted Christian monasteries. These were poorly defended, and the monks often had chests full of coins as well as precious crosses, plates and bells. Sometimes the Vikings attacked other ships. Like most pirates, they avoided damaging these ships too much, because they wanted to steal and use them themselves. When the Vikings returned home, they shared out the loot and boasted of their daring deeds.

3-second sum-up

The Vikings raided towns, villages and monasteries from the sea, taking people and treasure.

Famous Viking raids

789 CE The Isle of Portland in Wessex (southern England).

793 CE The monastery at Lindisfarne, Northumbria (northeastern England).

794 CE The monastery at Iona, off Scotland. It is attacked again in 795 CE, 802 CE and 806 CE.

795 CE Rathlin Island (off Antrim, Ireland) followed by the Irish kingdoms of Brega (798 CE) and Connacht (807 CE).

834–837 CE The Dutch town of Dorestad is destroyed four times.

834 CE The coastal defences of the Franks are attacked.

852 CE First attack on Wales – the island of Anglesey is hit in 903 CE and 918 CE.

Violent raids were not unusual in Europe in the 800s CE. The Vikings were the most successful raiders because they had the best ships and were the best seafarers.

Villagers were seized as slaves.

Christian monks would try to run away from the pagan Vikings. Some were killed with swords and axes.

Raiders looted buildings and set them on fire with a burning arrow. They wanted to drive out anyone who was hiding inside.

Cattle and sheep were rounded up.

Settlers overseas

... in 30 seconds

Viking raids mostly took place in summer months, when the sailing was best. But as the raiders grew bolder, they began to spend winters overseas as well. They set up onshore bases or camps and defended them from attack. The Irish called these longphorts.

Longphorts could be used as temporary centres for raiding expeditions, or as trading posts. Some of them grew into permanent settlements, into towns or even small kingdoms such as Dublin and Limerick in Ireland.

Ships would bring whole families and households to new settlements. They came with weapons and with tools to build homes and grow crops. Some women were captured on raids around the British Isles and taken to Iceland to be wives of new settlers. Sometimes the Viking settlers mixed in with people already living in the region.

Why did Vikings settle overseas? Many wanted better farmland than they had at home. Some could not inherit property of their own. A few may have been forced into exile because of crimes they had committed at home.

3-minute mission Norse detective

Vikings left traces of their language, Old Norse, in the names of islands, bays, towns and buildings across many parts of the world. Here are some examples. Can you use a map to find any more?

-ey or **-ay** = island e.g. Bardsey (Wales), Olney (USA)
-thwaite = meadow e.g. Le Thuit (France)
-ness = headland e.g. Inverness (Australia)
-by = settlement or farm e.g. Whitby (England), Grimsby (Canada)
-vik = bay e.g. Hoyvik (Faroe Islands), Reykjavik (Iceland)
-kirk = church e.g. Ormskirk (England), Falkirk (Scotland)

The settlers first built camps to live in before they made more permanent settlements.

Ships brought supplies and whole families ready to start new lives.

Swords and shields were kept to hand in case the settlers were attacked.

Vikings used local materials such as stone, timber and turf for building new homes.

Viking tent poles sometimes had decorative carvings.

Vikings chose sites that had good access to the sea, rivers and clean fresh water.

Raiders and fighters

In an age before guns or bombs, warriors fought closely, person to person, and combat was brutal. In reality, the Vikings were no more violent than other peoples of their time, such as the Franks or the Anglo-Saxons. But the Christian monks of the day described the Vikings as fiendish fighters. Later on, Norse writers wrote down exciting stories about the Vikings, called sagas. The sagas described the warriors as adventurous and heroic. For both of these reasons, the Vikings are still remembered as some of the most famous warriors in history.

Raiders and fighters
Glossary

battering ram A length of heavy timber used to smash through the defences of a fort or castle.

battle axe An axe designed for use as a weapon.

berserker A Viking warrior who went crazy during a battle, or a class or rank of warrior. Warriors wore the skin of a bear or wolf to gain the fighting power of an animal.

besiege To surround and cut off the enemy, so that they cannot receive supplies or get help.

boss A central stud on a shield, usually made of metal.

byrnie (brynja in Old Norse) A mail shirt, used as armour in battle.

catapult Any machine used in sieges to hurl missiles at the enemy.

close ranks To move nearer to each other while in a battle formation.

Danegeld Money raised by a king to pay off Viking invaders.

Danevirke An earthwork designed to protect the southern borders of Denmark from attack.

double-edged Of a sword, sharp on both edges of the blade.

gatehouse The defensive entrance to a fort or town.

hilt The handle of a sword.

housecarl (húskarl in Old Norse) A bodyguard or warrior of the royal household.

inlaid Decorated by filling in spaces with another material, such as a precious metal.

karl A free male citizen in Viking society, able to own property and trade.

mail A protective fabric made of small, interlinked metal rings.

Middle Ages/medieval The period of European history, which separates the time of Ancient Rome from the modern world of discovery and science. Some historians date it from 476 CE to 1453.

pitched battle A formal battle at a given place, as opposed to a skirmish or running conflict.

rampart A defensive wall or bank.

raven A large black crow, associated with the Norse god Odin.

refuge A place that is safe from attack, a haven.

ring fort In the Viking period, a system of defences used to encircle buildings.

saga Old Norse tales of adventures, voyages and battles.

shaft The long stick or pole that forms the body of a spear or arrow.

shield wall A defensive battle formation, in which warriors stood shoulder to shoulder with their shields overlapping.

steel Iron which has been mixed with a tiny amount of carbon, from charcoal, to form a very hard material. It was used to forge blades.

Warriors

... in 30 seconds

Viking warriors were mostly ordinary karls, who were called away from farming to go to war. Sometimes they joined up with other groups to form larger forces, but only a few were full-time, paid soldiers. Viking warriors might march to battle, sail there in ships or ride on horseback. Most of the fighting was on foot.

At the start of the battle, Viking archers might fire arrows at the enemy from powerful bows. Spears could be thrown or, as the fighters closed in on the enemy, used to jab and stab. Battle axes with curved blades were used to beat, hack or hook enemies, cracking open helmets or smashing shields. The Viking sword was double-edged with a groove. It was forged from iron and edged in steel, and was used to slash at the enemy.

We read about warriors who went really crazy in battle, but we don't know much about them. They worked themselves up into a furious rage. They are often called berserker a word suggesting that they wore shirts made of bearskin. However, some historians think that the word 'berserker' should properly refer to a top warrior or champion. Members of the king's personal bodyguard were called housecarls.

3-second sum-up

Most Viking men were part-time soldiers. They fought with bows, spears, axes and swords.

3-minute mission Name that sword

Weapons were valuable possessions, handed down from father to son. The sword of a king or a jarl might have a richly decorated hilt. An iron axe blade might be inlaid with silver. Vikings liked to give their best weapons nicknames, such as 'leg-biter', 'war-flame' or 'villain'. Can you make up some good names for a Viking sword?

Combat was exhausting. The fighters had to leap, kick, lunge and punch. All the time they were looking for an unguarded spot they could attack.

Sword blades were about 70–80 cm (28–32 in) long and edged in steel. Later Viking swords were longer.

A small axe weighed about 800 g (1.8 lbs).

Bows measured about 2 m (6 ft) and had a range of up to 250 m (275 yds). The arrows had iron heads.

Spears had a shaft (the handle) of ash wood and an iron head. They were 2–3 m (7–10 ft) long.

Battle-axes had curved blades and the wooden shaft could be long or short.

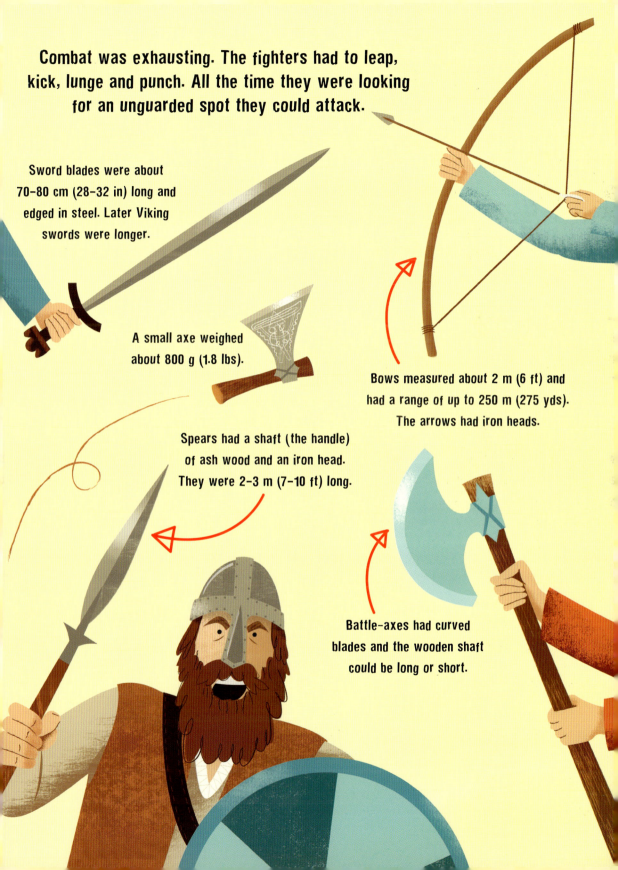

Armour

... in 30 seconds

In the early Middle Ages, few northern European warriors wore heavy armour to protect themselves in battle. Most men fought in their everyday clothes, wearing tunics and trousers. This gave them freedom to run and jump.

The richest Viking warriors might own a byrnie, a shirt of mail. This was made up of small interconnected iron rings. Each ring was linked to the four nearest to it.

Most iron helmets were round or conical, and padded inside with leather or sheepskin. They did not have horns, as shown so often in modern pictures! Some were fitted with a bar at the front, to protect the nose. The best helmets had a face guard, to protect the eyes and cheeks, or perhaps a mail fringe to cover the back of the neck.

Shields were used for defence, but could also be slammed into an opponent as a weapon of attack. They were made of wooden planks, rimmed and sometimes covered in leather. A central iron boss added strength and protected the hand-hold on the other side. Shields could be slung over the shoulder when not in use.

3-second sum-up

Viking armour included a simple iron helmet and, for those who could afford it, a mail shirt.

3-minute mission Make a shield

You need: • Heavy cardboard • Sticky tape • Coloured paints • Paintbrush

Viking shields were often painted in bright colours and bold patterns. Make a shield to fit your size by cutting out a large circle from heavy cardboard. Tape a cardboard handle on the back. On the front, paint the central boss in grey and around it add a coloured pattern, perhaps with swirls, quarters, stripes or a cross.

Warriors could defend a position by closing ranks and standing shoulder-to-shoulder, with their shields overlapping. This was called a shield wall. It was very hard for the enemy to break through it.

A mail shirt weighed about 12 kg (26 lbs). It had short sleeves and came down to the thigh.

Face guard

Nose bar

Leather rim

Shields were up to 1 m (3 ft) across and weighed about 5–7 kg (11–15 lbs).

Viking armies
... in 30 seconds

By the 840s CE, small groups of Viking raiders were joining up to fight in larger forces, perhaps numbering a thousand or more. These armies might be led by a king. Sometimes Viking armies joined up with one foreign kingdom in order to fight another.

Viking armies were able to march inland and fight pitched battles with their enemies. They attacked France in the 840s CE and the Anglo-Saxon kingdoms of England during the years 866 to 878 CE. They invaded, occupied and settled large areas of land.

Vikings in England and France found out that if they attacked the same place again and again, the enemy would give them money just to go away. In England this bribe later became known as Danegeld. The scheme never worked well for long for the defenders, because the Vikings would come back a few years later and demand even more.

Gradually, the enemies of the Vikings learned the best ways of fighting back. Alfred the Great, the Anglo-Saxon king of Wessex from 871 to 899 CE, greatly improved defences. He trained soldiers and built warships.

3-second sum-up

Vikings soon began to form large armies to attack cities, conquer new lands or demand money from their enemies.

3-minute mission Fly the raven banner

You need: • Small amount of fabric • Scissors • Fabric paints • Bamboo cane

Some Viking armies flew a small battle flag with a picture of a raven. This bird was an emblem of the great god Odin, the lord of battle and death. To make a flag, cut out a triangle shape from the fabric, with a curved lower edge. Make small cuts into the curved edge to create a fringe. Use fabric paints to draw the raven. Attach your battle flag to a bamboo cane.

Viking armies had enough warriors and weapons to attack or besiege places such as London, Paris, Ghent or Hamburg.

Ships on the river bring supplies to the Vikings.

This catapult can hurl boulders to knock down the city walls.

Wooden towers are set on fire with flaming arrows.

A battering ram can smash down the city gates.

Walls and forts

... in 30 seconds

Walls, ditches and fences were often built around towns to protect them from being attacked. Three hundred years before the Vikings, the Danes began work on a great wall – the Danevirke – to defend their homeland from attack by Franks and Saxons. This wall was made even better by Viking rulers, such as King Gudfred in 808 CE.

The Danevirke stretched for 30 km (19 miles) across Denmark, from the western wetlands to the eastern port of Hedeby, on the Baltic coast. In places it was up to 6 m (20 ft) high. It was still being used as a defence in warfare over 1,000 years later, in 1864, and its remains stand today.

During the reign of Harald Bluetooth (about 958 to 986 CE), the Vikings built ring forts in Denmark and southern Sweden. Wooden buildings and streets were surrounded by ditches and a circular mound, faced with heavy timbers, earth and stone. Each fort had gates in the north, south, east and west. The best known forts include Trelleborg and Fyrkat.

The Viking settlement at Dublin, Ireland, was protected by a bank made of mud and gravel, topped by a wooden fence. Later, the Vikings replaced this with a stone wall.

3-second sum-up

The Vikings built walls of earth, stone and timber along borders and around their towns and forts.

An island fortress

The old Viking sagas tell of an awesome island fortress called Jomsborg. It had stone towers defended by catapults and a harbour sealed off by a great iron gate. The Jomsvikings who lived there were a wild lot who hired out their services as warriors. Fact or fiction? Nobody can be sure, but some people believe the fortress did exist on the island of Wolin, in the southern Baltic Sea.

N

E

S

Vikings built ring forts to defend their towns and as places for the king's armies to be kept.

Timber-faced walls and ditches protected the people inside.

The walls had a gatehouse at the four points of a compass.

Ramparts

Guards

Messengers were sent on horseback to carry important news from the forts.

Forts may also have een gathering points or efuges in times of war, or used for collecting taxes in peacetime.

Everyday life

Away from the dangers of battle or the ocean waves, life carried on as normal for most Vikings. There were seasonal tasks to carry out on the farm, daily household chores, buying and selling at market and babies to care for. The Vikings loved life, but it was a hard struggle for them. Almost everything had to be made by hand, and a lot of the work required hard graft and muscle power. If you had an accident or became ill, there were no life-saving medicines or hospitals either – just herbal remedies, or a charm to bring good luck.

Everyday life
Glossary

anvil The heavy iron block on which a smith hammers hot metal into shape.

bellows A machine that puffs a blast of air into a fire, to make it burn more strongly.

cesspit A hole dug in the soil to dispose of sewage.

felt A fabric made by compacting wool fibres.

forge A smithy, a place for shaping and hammering hot metal.

griddle A flat, heated surface used for cooking.

hnefatafl A popular Viking boardgame. The name literally means fist-table, but the game is better known as king's-table. To pronounce it, see page 92.

kenning A poetic or alternative description of something or someone, which avoids using the normal term.

leg bindings Long narrow strips of cloth, sometimes wrapped around the leg and foot by Viking men.

linen A textile made from fibres of the flax plant.

loom The frame on which a textile is woven.

madder A plant with small yellow flowers, but with a long root used in preparing red dyes.

mead An alcoholic drink made from honey and water.

midden A rubbish tip.

Middle Ages/medieval The period of European history that separates the time of ancient Rome from the modern world of discovery and science. Some historians date it from 476 to 1453 CE.

preserve To prepare food so that it remains edible, by drying, smoking, salting or pickling.

saga A Norse story written down in the Middle Ages, telling of families, feuds, great sea voyages and adventures.

sedge A group of rush-like wetland plants.

shift A woman's dress or an under-dress, simple and unwaisted.

smithy A smith's workshop, where metal is hammered and forged.

soapstone A type of rock that is easy to carve. The Vikings used it to make cooking pots.

tanner Someone who soaks and treats animal hides to turn them into leather.

tapestry A textile woven as a work of art, usually hung on a wall for display.

walrus ivory The long, tusk-like upper teeth of the walrus, used as a material from which objects were carved in the Viking period.

wattle and daub A building material made of interwoven wooden strips plastered with materials such as wet clay, dung and straw.

weld A plant also known as dyer's rocket, with yellow-green flowers. It produces a bright yellow dye.

welding Joining together two pieces of metal, by heating, pressing and hammering.

wick A strip of fibre inside a candle or oil lamp, which soaks up the fuel and burns.

woad A plant with yellow flowers. Its leaves produce a blue dye.

How to dress

... in 30 seconds

Viking clothes for men and women were colourful, and their fashions changed over time, too. Viking women and girls generally wore a long shift of linen, and over that a shorter dress or pinafore made of wool. This was held up by shoulder straps and fastened by brooches.

Glass or amber beads could hang in a loop between the two brooches. Keys, scissors or other useful items were hung from a belt at the waist. A shawl, a cloak or a fur might be worn on a cold night. Young girls wore their hair long and sometimes braided, or with combs made from antler horn. Married women wore their hair in a bun, under a headscarf.

Men and boys wore a tunic of linen under an outer tunic of wool, often trimmed with fancy braid. Trousers could be baggy or narrow, and sometimes leg bindings were wrapped around the calves. There were hooded cloaks, caps of wool and fur hats. Men wore their hair long, and were expected to have a beard and moustache, kept neatly trimmed.

3-minute mission Make a brooch

A high-status Viking woman wore the very best brooches to show just how rich she was. Two oval brooches of bronze decorated the shoulder straps, while smaller brooches fastened cloaks and shawls. You can cut out brooch shapes from stiff card and paint with Viking animal designs from the Internet. Tape a safety pin to the back and wear with pride!

Spinning, weaving and sewing were carried out by women in the home. Textiles were woven on a large, upright loom.

Linen shift

Woollen dress

Hair pin

Head scarf

Brooch to fasten shoulder straps

Children wear the same sort of clothing as their parents, just in smaller sizes.

Linen tunic

Woollen tunic

Woollen trousers

Fur hat

Leather shoes, boots or slippers are made of calfskin or goatskin, and often worn with woollen socks.

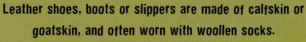

Farming life
... in 30 seconds

In Viking times there were few proper roads. People walked along rough tracks through the countryside. Some rode small, tough horses, or used them for carrying packs of goods. There were wooden wagons, and in winter, travellers could use sledges, skates or skis.

Most Vikings lived by farming the land. In warmer areas where the soil was good, the farms were quite near to each other, sometimes forming villages. In colder regions with poor soil, there were fewer farms.

Farming settlements were home to land-owning families, free labourers and slaves. The main building was the longhouse (see pages 56–57). Around it there might be a wash-house, barns, cowsheds, a dairy and a smithy.

Viking farmers grew rye, barley and oats, which could be ground into flour with a round stone. In warmer regions they could plant wheat. Hay was grown to feed the animals. Cattle grazed on fresh grass on the hillsides during the summer. In autumn they were brought down to the cow sheds. People could preserve meats by drying, salting or smoking them.

3-minute mission What's it for?

All these tools might be found on a Viking farm. What do you think they were used for?

1. Sickle   2. Shears   3. Quern

3-second sum-up

Farmers raised cattle, sheep and pigs, and grew crops such as rye, barley and oats.

See page 96 for answers.

Throughout the year, most Vikings spent their time looking after their animals and crops on farms.

In spring, farmers planted seeds of rye, barley and oats.

In summer, the sheep were sheared to provide wool for clothing.

In autumn, the crops were harvested.

In the cold days of winter, cattle were kept in sheds or at one end of the longhouse and fed on hay.

Inside a longhouse
... in 30 seconds

At the centre of the farmstead stood the longhouse, perhaps 30 to even 60 m (32 to 66 yds) long, and 5 to 7 m (16 to 23 ft) wide. It was normally built from timber, with walls made of criss-crossed sticks plastered with mud or dung ('wattle and daub'). The roof was thatched with straw or tiled with wood. In areas where wood was scarce, such as Iceland, the longhouse might be stone-built, with a roof of turf. As time passed, extra rooms might be added at the sides.

Indoors, rows of wooden posts held up the roof beams, dividing the hall into three aisles. The floor was made of packed soil and ash. The centre of family life was the hearth. This was a firepit, which provided heating, light and cooking. Smoke escaped through holes in the roof.

Wooden benches or ledges in the side aisles were used as seats and beds. Mattresses were filled with straw or feathers, and blankets or furs kept sleepers warm when winter storms roared over the roof. There was little furniture but shields could be hung on the walls, and a wealthy landowner might decorate the walls with carvings or tapestries.

3-second sum-up

The longhouse was the centre of family life, used for eating, sleeping and tasks such as weaving.

Lamplight

It was dark inside a longhouse as there were no windows. Only a little light came from the fire, so the Vikings needed to use lamps. Simple lamps were made from stone containers filled with oil extracted from plants or from fish, seals or whales. The wick was made of cottongrass, a kind of sedge, which burned steadily. Modern oil lamps are based on the same idea.

A longhouse needed to be big to fit in a family, their relatives or guests and farm workers. One end was sometimes also used to house farm animals in winter.

This ironing board is made of whalebone. Clothes are smoothed out with a ball of glass.

Chests, baskets, barrels, buckets and hooks were used for storage.

The roof was covered with thatch or turf.

Cauldrons were made of iron and hung on chains over the fire.

Mattresses were filled with straw or feathers.

Weaving area

Walls were made of wattle (criss-crossed sticks), which were plastered with daub (mud or straw mix) in between strong wooden posts.

Peat, brushwood or logs were burnt in the firepit.

Cooking area

Food and feasts

... in 30 seconds

Family meals were taken mid-morning and in the evening. Oats, barley or rye were used to make porridge or a coarse bread, which could be baked on an iron or stone griddle. Cheese was made from the milk of sheep, goats and cows.

Leeks, onions, turnips, cabbages and peas were grown in the fields. Herrings were a big part of the diet, whether freshly caught, smoked or salted. Honey was used to sweeten meals. Meat might be roasted, but more often it was boiled or stewed. Beef, pork, mutton, goat or chicken were all eaten. Even horse meat was eaten until the Vikings became Christian, when it was banned because it was associated with Pagan festivals.

Hunting in the woods and fields brought in hare, deer, elk, boar and wildfowl, and useful plant foods such as nettles, berries and nuts. The eggs of seabirds were collected from cliffs.

The Vikings ate from bowls or plates made of wood, using knives or daggers, and spoons made of wood or horn – but no forks. Their dishes were made from a type of rock called soapstone. Pottery cups and jugs were often imported from Germany, along with wine.

3-second sum-up

The Viking diet included coarse bread, stewed vegetables, fish and meat.

3-minute mission Viking snacks

We don't have any Viking recipes as such, but we do know which foods they ate. Your mission is to prepare some healthy food for a hungry Viking friend! In a bowl, mix up some oats, apple slices, blueberries, hazelnuts, milk and honey. On the side you could provide a wholemeal bun with some goats' cheese. Ask your friend to eat it using a spoon!

Chiefs or jarls liked to entertain guests and enjoyed feasting and drinking. A seasonal festival or a family celebration could last for days.

Drinking horn

'Ves heil' means 'Your good health!' in Old Norse.

Barley bread

Meat was usually boiled or stewed.

Cheese

Fruit

Eggs

Herring and vegetables were often eaten.

Soapstone dishes

Wooden cup

Wooden plate

Strong drinks included ale, made from barley, and mead, made from honey. Wine was imported from Germany.

Living in a town

... in 30 seconds

In much of Europe, big cities had been built by the Romans. Regions such as Scandinavia, though, which lay outside the Roman empire, did not develop a city lifestyle. Instead, smaller but busy towns such as Hedeby, Germany, which had a population of about 1,000 – 2,000, grew up from the 700s and 800s CE.

Viking towns were often sea or river ports, and were centres for making and trading goods. Inside the town's defences, the streets were paved with lengths of heavy timber. There were market stalls, probably selling everything from fresh fish to hammers and nails. Ships were moored at jetties in the harbour.

Houses were thatched, and built of timber beams with walls of planking or wattle and daub. They were similar inside to a longhouse. Some buildings had sunken cellars, which were probably used as warehouses or workshops. Household rubbish was tipped onto middens, and sewage was buried in cesspits. There was no proper drainage.

3-second sum-up

Viking towns were small but busy centres of craft and trade. Many of them were ports.

Timeline: Viking towns

700s CE Ribe is founded, a trading centre in Jutland. It still exists and is Denmark's oldest town.

750s CE Birka in Sweden becomes the western end of trade routes into Russia. Today it is Sweden's oldest town.

780s CE Kaupang is a centre of craft and trade in Norway. The name means 'market place'. Aarhus is founded at about the same time.

804 CE The first mention of Hedeby, on the border between Danish and German lands.

870 CE Viking settlers found Reykjavík, the capital of Iceland.

Towns often started as busy ports and began to grow larger in the 800s CE. A few survived and became the big cities of today.

The land was fenced off into plots, with sheds, gardens and farm animals.

Jetty

Streets were paved with timber.

Traders and market stalls

There were no windows but holes in the roof let out smoke.

Front doors faced the street.

A typical town house measured about 12 by 5 m (39 by 16 ft), but a rich merchant's house could be much bigger.

Growing up

... in 30 seconds

You needed to be lucky to grow up at all in the early Middle Ages. Many mothers died giving birth, and infants often died from illnesses that could not be cured. At the Viking settlement of Jórvik (York, in England), probably one in three babies never reached adulthood.

Nine days after the birth, the father placed the baby on his knee and sprinkled the head with water. He or she was given a name and recognized as a member of the family. Guests brought gifts to the ceremony.

Boys and girls were expected to work hard. They would help on the farm or in the workshop, spinning wool, mending clothes, looking after younger siblings or animals, fishing or cutting wood. There were no schools or formal lessons. Children might be fostered out to another family, to strengthen social ties or to learn a new skill.

At 12 a boy was already taking on adult tasks, and at 15 he could go off raiding. A girl would marry in her early teens. Marriages were generally arranged as business deals or alliances between families.

3-second sum-up

Viking children had no schools to go to. They liked to play games, but were expected to work very hard.

3-minute mission Make a bouncy felt ball

You need: • Some wool strands • A bowl • Washing up liquid

1. Mix 4 tablespoons of washing-up liquid with 6 cups of warm water in a bowl.
2. Screw up a small ball of woollen fibre with your hand, then wind strands around it. When your ball is twice as big as the one you want, dip it in the water. Keep rolling it between the palms of your hands for 10 minutes, without squeezing.
3. When it has shrunk, rinse it under a cold tap and let it dry. Tie some coloured woollen yarn around it – and let it bounce!

Viking children had to grow up quickly and learn skills such as swimming, farm work and sword fighting, to help them set up new communities when they grew up.

Toddlers played with dolls, toy animals or balls made of felt.

Young children fought with pretend swords made of wood to prepare for real sword fights.

As children got older, they were expected to work hard in the longhouse and on the farm.

By the age of 15, boys were old enough to go off on raids.

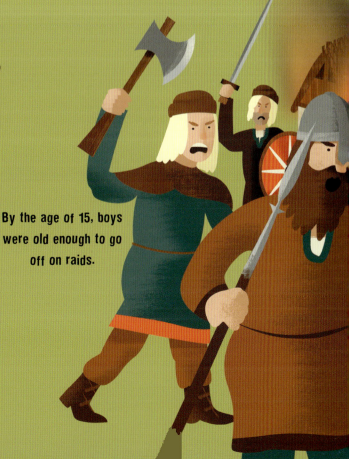

Girls got married once they reached their early teens.

Fun and games
... in 30 seconds

Men loved sports such as wrestling, tug-of-war, weight-lifting, skating and swimming. There were bat-and-ball games, too. Most sports were played to the extreme and often ended in violence.

Boardgames were always very popular. Viking families played dice, chess, draughts and games similar to backgammon. One game was called 'hnefatafl'. Players had to protect their king while he tried to escape to his corner castles.

Little is known about how the Vikings danced or played music, but we do know that they played pipes and flutes made from bone or horn, and stringed instruments including a harp. Ibrahim al-Tartushi, a traveller from Spain, visited Hedeby in 965. He said that Viking songs sounded like dogs or wild animals howling!

The Vikings loved words, especially riddles, rhymes and poems. Travelling poets called skalds would attend the feast of a jarl or a king and compose verse to music. In the long winter evenings, stories were told around the fire of gods, giants, tricksters, trolls, heroes and kings. Later in the Middle Ages, longer stories called sagas were written down in books.

3-second sum-up

The Vikings liked extreme outdoor sports as well as boardgames, music and storytelling.

3-minute mission Word puzzles

Viking poets liked to use kennings – phrases that described something without directly saying what it was. The listener had to work out the meaning. The sun might be called a 'sky-candle'. The wind might be called a 'tree-breaker'. Can you make up some modern kennings? For example, a motorcycle could be a 'fast-lane snarler'. How about inventing a kenning for a smartphone?

Vikings liked to entertain themselves with music, singing, wrestling and playing boardgames.

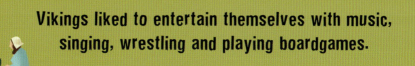

Wrestling was a popular sport but it could get violent.

Scandinavian music of the early Middle Ages was not written down. It remains a mystery.

Horn

Flute

Stringed instrument

These Viking chess pieces were found on the Isle of Lewis in Scotland. They were carved from walrus ivory in the 1100s CE.

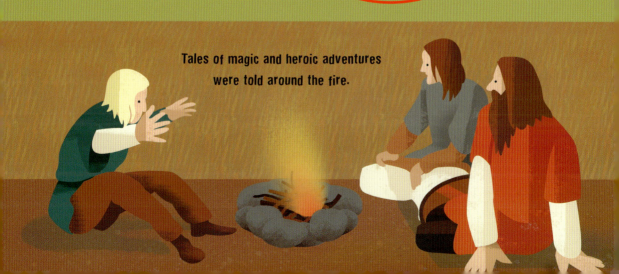

Tales of magic and heroic adventures were told around the fire.

Arts and crafts

... in 30 seconds

In the days before factories, it was individual craft workers who made the things that people used, bought or sold every day. In a Viking town there might be carpenters, tanners of leather, shoemakers and glassmakers. Woodturners used lathes to shape wooden bowls and poles. At home, potters made jugs, pots, loom weights and oil lamps.

A smith worked with metal and was probably the most important craft worker of all. He worked in a forge, using bellows to make the furnace burn hot, so that the metal could be shaped into nails, knives, axes, keys, pots and pans. Swordsmiths might take a week or more to fashion a blade, twisting iron rods, welding and hammering.

Other metalworkers and jewellers used precious materials such as silver or gold. They worked with beautiful glass and amber beads to make rings, necklaces and bracelets.

Carvers worked on all sorts of surfaces, such as horn, walrus ivory, whale tooth, antler or soapstone. Carved wood decorated houses, furniture, ships, wagons and, later, churches. Favourite Viking patterns included interlaced knots and loops, birds and fish, beasts and dragons. These designs influenced those of other peoples such as the Anglo-Saxons and the Irish.

3-second sum-up

Craftworkers made tools, weapons and household goods as well as beautiful carvings and delicate jewellery.

Bright colours

Viking textiles and tapestries were brightly coloured with dyes made from plants. The leaves of the woad plant turned cloth blue. The husks of walnuts produced a brown. The root of a plant called madder made things red. The flowers of weld, or dyer's rocket, gave a yellow dye, while heather stems were used for dark green.

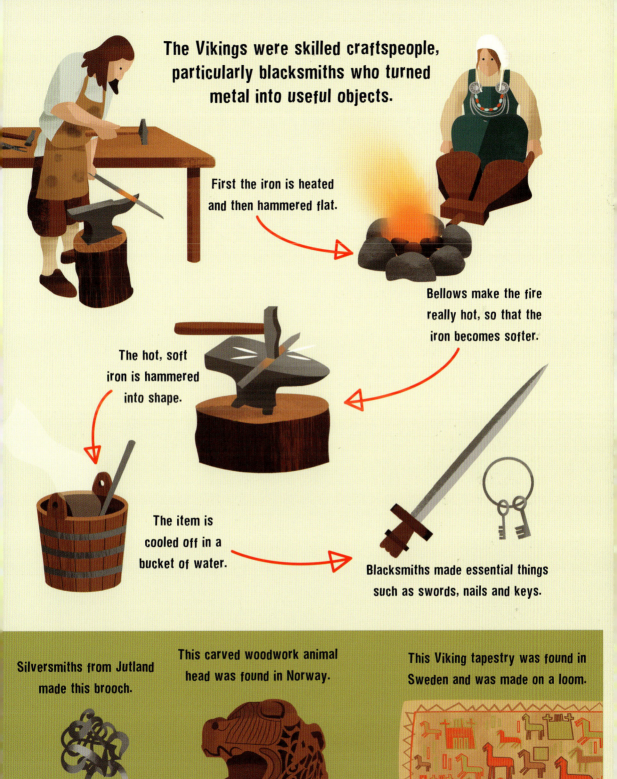

The Vikings were skilled craftspeople, particularly blacksmiths who turned metal into useful objects.

First the iron is heated and then hammered flat.

Bellows make the fire really hot, so that the iron becomes softer.

The hot, soft iron is hammered into shape.

The item is cooled off in a bucket of water.

Blacksmiths made essential things such as swords, nails and keys.

Silversmiths from Jutland made this brooch.

This carved woodwork animal head was found in Norway.

This Viking tapestry was found in Sweden and was made on a loom.

Religion and beliefs

Before the Vikings became Christian, they had myths to explain the origins of the world and the meaning of life and death. The Vikings believed there was a human world (Midgard) and a home of the gods (Asgard) connected by a shimmering rainbow bridge, called Bifröst. In all there were nine such worlds inhabited by humans and all sorts of other beings, such as gods, elves, dwarfs, giants and dragons. This universe was held together by the roots of a gigantic ash tree called Yggdrasil. These old myths and legends survived even after Christianity came to the Viking lands, in the 800s CE.

Religion and beliefs
Glossary

Aesir One of the two groups of Norse gods. The Aesir included **Odin** and **Thor**.

Asgard The home of the **Aesir** gods, one of the nine worlds of Norse mythology.

Baldr A god associated with love, peace, justice and the sun; the son of **Odin** and the goddess **Frigg**.

burial mound A pile of earth marking a tomb or grave.

Freyja A goddess of love and beauty; the twin sister of **Freyr**.

Freyr A fertility god of the **Vanir**, who lives in Álfheim, the world of the elves.

Frigg A powerful goddess of wisdom; the wife of **Odin**.

Landvaettir Spirits of the countryside and nature.

Loki A god known for making mischief, who can change shape and take the form of an animal.

Midgard In Norse myths, the middle world where human beings live.

missionary Someone sent to spread a religious message and convert people to their faith.

myth An ancient tale of gods, goddesses, heroes or monsters, heaven or hell. It aims to explain the meaning of life or why things happen as they do.

Norns Female beings who visit babies to decide how their lives will work out in the future.

Odin The greatest and the most powerful of the **Aesir** gods. Odin is the god of battle, death, healing and knowledge.

pagan A person who follows a pre-Christian or non-Christian faith.

pyre A large open wood fire, used to burn bodies during a funeral.

sacrifice Killing an animal or a person as an offering to a god or gods.

solstice When the Sun is at its greatest distance from the equator – in the summer, this is the longest day of the year and in the winter, it is the shortest.

stave church A stave is a strip of wood. Stave churches, made of timber planks and tiled with wood, were made by the first Christians in Scandinavia.

superstitious Believing in supernatural causes being responsible for everyday events.

Thor A god of the **Aesir**, linked with thunder and lightning. The son of **Odin**, he fights giants with his hammer.

Valhalla (Valhöll in Old Norse) **Odin's** great hall in **Asgard**, the home of warriors killed in battle.

Vanir One of the two groups of Norse gods, including **Freyr** and **Freyja**. After a war, the Vanir became a sub-group of the **Aesir**.

Yggdrasil In Norse myths, the great ash tree that supports the nine worlds of the universe.

Yule (Jól in Old Norse) The pagan winter festival of the Vikings and other Germanic peoples. It later became taken over by Christmas.

Gods and goddesses
... in 30 seconds

According to some Norse myths, there were originally two tribes of gods and goddesses. The Aesir were associated with power and war and the Vanir were associated with wisdom, nature, magic and fertility. The two tribes fought each other before they joined together.

The chief of the gods was called Odin and he belonged to the Aesir. He only had one eye and rode across the stormy sky on his eight-legged horse Sleipnir. He owned two wolves called Geri and Freki. His two ravens, Hugin and Munin, flew around the world to bring him news. Odin lived in a great hall called Valhöll. Warriors who died bravely in battle were taken there to feast with the gods.

The most popular god was red-headed Thor, the thunderer, who wielded a mighty war hammer. Freyr and Freyja were twins, the god and goddess of fertility and love. Baldr was god of the summer sun. Nothing could injure him, except an arrow made from mistletoe wood. His blind brother killed him with one. As usual, one god was at the root of this trouble – Loki, the mischief maker.

3-second sum-up

The Viking gods and goddesses included the great Odin, Thor the god of thunder and Freyja the goddess of love.

3-minute mission Days of the week

In English and some other languages, some days of the week are still named after the old Viking and Germanic gods. See if you can work out which day of the week is named after these:

Anglo-Saxon god	Norse god	Day
Woden	Odin	?
Tiw	Tyr	?
Frige	Frigg	?
Thunre (Thunder)	Thor	?

See page 96 for answers.

Here are some of the many Viking gods and goddesses:

Gungnir was Odin's magic spear that never missed its target.

Odin had two ravens.

Sleipnir was Odin's eight-legged horse.

Odin had two wolves Geri and Freki.

Odin was chief of the gods.

Thor was the god of thunder.

Loki was the mischief maker.

Thor's hammer Mjöllnir was forged by dwarves.

Freyr and Freyja, the god and goddess of fertility and love.

The cats Bygul and Trjegul pulled Freyja's chariot.

Freyja had a boar called Hildisvini.

Customs and festivals

... in 30 seconds

The Vikings' belief in spirits, gods and goddesses was rooted in everyday life. The goddess Frigg ruled over weddings and marriage. That was why Vikings got married on Frigg's Day, or Friday. It was also thought that the fate of humans was decided at birth, by female beings called Norns.

The Vikings sometimes sacrificed animals and even humans to please the gods. Some religious rituals may have taken place outdoors, beside special trees or rocks, or in wooden buildings.

Vikings celebrated the passing of the seasons with sacrifices, feasting, drinking and fire festivals. Later, the Christian church took over many old pagan customs, adapting them to the new faith. When the midwinter festival of Yule (Jól) was replaced by Christmas, Vikings carried on bringing a great log of oak into the house to start the New Year's fire. We still decorate our houses with plants at Christmas time, as the Vikings did long ago.

It is thought the Vikings celebrated May Day and Midsummer Day, too. In Sweden, people continue the May Day tradition by lighting bonfires and singing songs to welcome the return of warmth and light.

3-second sum-up

The Vikings held seasonal festivals, marked by sacrifices, feasting and fire, some of which still survive today.

3-minute mission Lucky charms

You need: • Self-drying clay • Silver paint • Paintbrush • String

The Vikings believed that wearing charms, such as a 'Thor's hammer' symbol or an image of the goddess Freyja, would bring good luck. Make your own hammer (see drawing above) or a Freyja figure from clay. Leave a hole so that you can string it around your neck. Paint it silver when dry.

The Vikings held festivals throughout the year to honour their spirits, gods and goddesses.

In the winter, Vikings decorated their houses with evergreen plants.

In midsummer, Vikings may have made bonfires to celebrate the solstice. They would sing songs and dance.

In autumn, animal sacrifice, known as a blot, took place to please the gods.

Viking funerals

... in 30 seconds

Death was never far away in the Viking period. Disease, warfare and giving birth meant that many people died young. Those men and women who survived into their fifties were considered old.

Funerals varied greatly between regions and from one period to the next. Some Vikings were cremated on open fires or pyres after they died. Most were buried in the earth, in simple graves or under a mound.

Vikings were often buried with their possessions, so they would have everything they might need in their next life. The grave of one smith contained all the hammers and tongs from his forge. The rich and powerful were given their best weapons or their finest clothes and jewellery. Some were buried with the sacrificed bodies of their slaves, and animals such as horses and dogs.

Kings and queens were sometimes buried in finely carved wagons with their best horses, or in beautiful longships. It isn't known whether these were seen as transport to other worlds, or just as impressive symbols of worldly wealth and power.

3-second sum-up

Vikings were cremated or buried in the earth along with their favourite things.

The Oseberg ship

A beautiful ship was excavated by archaeologists in Norway over 100 years ago. It had lain buried under a mound of earth since the year 843 CE. It was made of oak and decorated with carvings. Inside were the skeletons of two women, one in a very fine dress and linen veil. Also in the ship were richly carved sleighs and a wagon, a bed post, textiles and tapestries.

Vikings were often buried with their possessions in simple graves or under a mound.

In some places stones were placed around the grave in the shape of a ship.

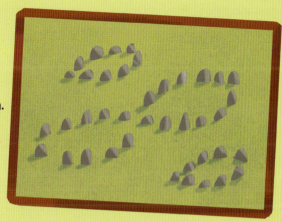

Burial mounds were later seen as spooky places. People were afraid they might meet the spirits of the undead.

Rich Vikings were buried with everything they might need in their next life.

The coming of Christianity

... in 30 seconds

By the start of the Viking age, most people in western Europe had become followers of the Christian faith and believed in the teachings of Jesus Christ, but Vikings still held on to their own beliefs. These religious differences sometimes caused trading disputes and battles.

Many Vikings who had settled overseas soon became Christian. Some thought the Christian God brought prosperity and good fortune. Some were forced to convert after they had been defeated in battle. In the 700s and 800s CE Christian missionaries travelled to Scandinavia to preach the new faith and build churches.

For many years pagan and Christian beliefs existed side by side in the Viking lands. Some new Christians still prayed to Thor in an emergency. King Harald Bluetooth, who ruled from Jelling, in Denmark, became a Christian in 960 CE. Later pictures show him being baptized in a barrel of water, by a monk called Poppo. During the 1000s CE Christianity spread through the Viking lands, but some people resisted and still made sacrifices to the old gods.

3-second sum-up

The Christian religion took about 300 years to take the place of the old pagan beliefs of the Vikings.

Pagan beliefs today

Viking settlers in Iceland believed that the countryside was protected by spirits known as Landvaettir, who lived in the rocks and fields. People said that the Landvaettir hated violence, so longship chiefs approaching Iceland would take down their dragon heads so as not to upset them. Belief in these spirits still exists today, and Icelanders protect particular sites from being disturbed by builders or farm workers. Four Landvaettir 'protectors' appear on the back of modern Icelandic coins and Iceland's coat-of-arms.

Missionaries spread Christianity across Viking lands, though some Vikings held on to their pagan beliefs.

828 CE

The Christian missionary Ansgar visits Birka, Sweden.

960 CE

The Danish King Harald Bluetooth becomes a Christian.

1000 CE

The lawspeaker in Iceland judged that Christianity should be adopted (after thinking about it for a day under a cloak), but allowed people to carry on practising the pagan religion.

995 CE

King Olaf Tryggvason builds the first church in Norway. He tries to force his people to convert to Christianity.

Christianity spreads in Norway under King Olaf II.

1015 CE

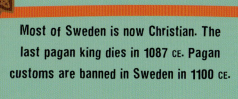

Most of Sweden is now Christian. The last pagan king dies in 1087 CE. Pagan customs are banned in Sweden in 1100 CE.

The wider world

The proof that the Vikings had been great travellers and settlers can be found in the hoards of Viking treasure that are still being discovered today. They include coins, jewellery, gold and silver. Sometimes these items had been traded legally, but often they had been looted during raiding. One hoard was found in a bog at Hoen, Norway, in 1834. It contained items from France, Russia, England, the Byzantine empire and the lands of the Arabs. The Spillings Hoard, found in Sweden in 1999, included 14,295 coins, which were mostly from Muslim lands.

The wider world
Glossary

Danelaw The area of Anglo-Saxon England that was taken over, settled and governed by the Vikings.

dynasty A family in which rule or power is handed down from one generation to the next.

elite A superior or special group of people with high social standing.

Frankish Of the Franks, a people living in France during the early Middle Ages. They gave their name to the country.

hoard A secret store of money or valuable objects.

housecarl (húskarl in Old Norse) A bodyguard or warrior of the royal household.

Inuit A people of Arctic North America. Archaeologists describe such peoples living there in Viking times as belonging to the Dorset and Thule cultures. The Vikings called them 'skraelings'.

legacy Something that has been handed down from the past to later generations.

Markland An area of the North American coast, probably Labrador in Canada, identified by Leif Eiriksson.

mercenary A soldier who hires himself out, fighting for money.

Miklagard The Vikings' name for Constantinople (Istanbul). It means 'the great city'.

Rus A people who traded and built up new towns in Eastern Europe, giving their name to Russia. They may have been Vikings or Slavs.

Up Helly Aa A winter fire festival held in Shetland, off Scotland, celebrating the memory of Viking settlement.

Varangian Guard An elite guard founded in 988 CE to protect the Byzantine emperors. It was mostly made up of Vikings, but with some Anglo-Saxons and Germans.

Varangians The name given to Vikings from Sweden by the Slavs and the Greeks.

Vinland An area of the North American coast, probably Newfoundland in Canada, identified by Leif Eiriksson.

Western Europe

... in 30 seconds

The Vikings reached many parts of western Europe to trade, settle or do battle. Few rivers, islands or coasts around the North Sea, the Irish Sea or the Channel were safe from their dragon ships.

The Vikings' largest area of settlement was across central and northern England, which became known as the Danelaw. Southern Anglo-Saxon cities such as London were also attacked. After 1016 CE, under King Cnut, England became, for a time, part of the Danish empire. In 1066 CE Harald Hardrada, King of Norway, tried to invade England but was defeated.

The lands that are now called Germany, France, the Netherlands and Belgium were also plagued by Viking attacks. The Vikings besieged Paris in 845 CE and again in 885–886 CE. In despair, the Frankish kings gave away the region of Normandy to the Viking chief Hrólfr or Rollo in 911 CE. Brittany was also attacked by Vikings time after time.

The Vikings sailed down stormy Atlantic coasts and into the warm, blue waters of the Mediterranean Sea. They attacked Seville and other cities in Muslim Spain. In the 860s CE, a Viking fleet captured the island of Sicily.

3-second sum-up

The Vikings overran large areas of Britain and Ireland and attacked the mainland and the islands of western Europe.

Raids and invasions in western Europe

780s–790s CE France and England raided.

830s CE Viking attacks on the Netherlands. The first of many raids on London, England.

840s CE Raids in Scotland and Ireland, the settlement at Dublin. Attacks on Portugal and Spain, raiding the Muslim city of Seville. Major assualts on Hamburg and Paris.

860s CE Italy raided. Large areas of England are settled.

885–886 CE Northern France attacked, and Paris is besieged.

1013 CE Sweyn Forkbeard invades England.

Viking raiding and settlement was at its most intense in northwestern Europe, but their fleets also sailed along Atlantic and Mediterranean coasts.

Scandinavia

They fought with the peoples of England and Ireland.

Scots and Picts

North Sea

Gaels

Anglo-Saxons

· Dublin

· Hamburg

Atlantic Ocean

· London

They attacked northern France and beseiged Paris.

Frankish warrior

The Vikings traded and fought with many other people living in northern Europe at that time.

Western Europe

Bay of Biscay

They fought with Moorish warriors in Muslim Spain.

· Cordoba

· Seville

North Atlantic

... in 30 seconds

The Vikings sailed west and reached the Faroe Islands, which are north of Scotland, in about 800 CE. They settled here to fish and raise sheep. In 874 CE Norse seafarers sailed on further to Iceland. The only previous settlers there had been a few Irish monks. The newcomers built farms on the best land and fished the seas. They loved to tell stories in the Icelandic language.

A seafarer called Gunnbjörn Ulfsson, who had been blown off course in a storm, was the first Viking to sight Greenland. This huge Arctic island was first settled permanently by Eirik the Red in about 982 CE. He called it Greenland to attract more settlers, but really it was a bleak and icy place inhabited by scattered Inuit communities. Settlers scraped a living by farming and hunting seals.

In about 1003 CE Eirik's son Leif 'the Lucky' sailed to the mainland of North America and landed at Labrador, which he called 'Markland', and Newfoundland, or 'Vinland'. The Vikings bartered goods and sometimes fought with the North American tribes who lived there. Remains of Viking buildings and artefacts have been found at L'Anse aux Meadows, in the north of Newfoundland.

3-second sum-up

The Vikings sailed westwards to the Faroe Islands, Iceland, Greenland, Labrador and Newfoundland.

Raids and invasions in the far north

800 CE Vikings settle on the Faroe Islands.

874 CE Vikings explore and settle Iceland.

982 CE Eirik 'the Red' settles at Brattahlid, in Greenland.

c.986 CE Seafarer Bjarni Herjolfsson sights the mainland coast of North America.

1000s CE Leif Eiriksson 'the Lucky' explores Labrador.

Viking explorers settled in Iceland and the Faroe Islands and reached North America over a thousand years ago.

Newfoundland in North America, Greenland and Iceland.

The Faroes and Iceland remained permanent Scandinavian settlements but some, like Greenland, were abandoned by 1408 CE.

In North America, the Vikings fought with the Native American tribes but also exchanged goods.

Eastern lands

... in 30 seconds

Swedish Vikings sailed across the Baltic Sea to raid the coast of Finland. They travelled into Russia, to Lake Ladoga and Novgorod. They traded in furs, amber, beeswax, honey and slaves. They rowed down the great rivers of central and eastern Europe, to the Black Sea. The Greeks and Slavs called these Vikings 'Varangians'.

Some historians believe that a people known as the Rus, who gave their name to Russia, were Varangians. Their legendary chieftain, Rurik, is said to have founded a royal dynasty in 862 CE. Other historians disagree, but it is clear that both Varangians and Slavs helped to shape the future of eastern Europe.

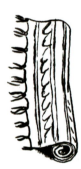

Varangians travelled to the Caspian Sea and overland to Baghdad. From there, trading routes stretched eastwards all the way to China. The northerners traded with the Arabs for textiles and silver.

In the 900s CE some Vikings hired themselves out as mercenaries, to protect the Byzantine emperors. They were known as the Varangian Guard and they became an elite force, taking part in many famous battles and adventures. They were based at Constantinople (previously Byzantium and now modern-day Istanbul), which they called 'the great city' – Miklagard.

3-second sum-up

The Vikings travelled into eastern Europe, traded in the markets of the Middle East and fought for the Byzantine emperors.

Raids and invasions in the east

800s CE The town of Birka in Sweden is the start of trading routes in eastern Europe and Asia.

859 CE Novgorod in Russia is a major trading centre for the Swedish Vikings or 'Varangians'.

862 CE Rurik founds a royal dynasty, which rules a large state called Kievan Rus.

911 CE Varangians fight as mercenaries for the Byzantines.

The Swedish Vikings moved eastwards into Finland and Russia, and from there southwards into Asia.

Finland and Russia

The Vikings traded in...

amber

silver

fur

slaves

They rowed down rivers to trade with Arabs.

Some Vikings hired themselves out as mercenaries.

End of the Viking age

... in 30 seconds

During the 1000s CE, Europe was going through many changes. Small kingdoms and territories were uniting under powerful kings. The Vikings were becoming Christian. Danes, Norwegians and Swedes went on to play an important part in European history, but many Viking settlements overseas became swallowed up by new kingdoms such as England, France or Scotland.

In France, the Normans still showed some of the old Viking spirit though. They sailed off to conquer Sicily and southern Italy, and in 1066 CE they crossed the Channel to conquer England.

The Normans built great castles, and new warriors called knights, who were heavily armoured and on horseback, were used to defend them instead of the housecarls fighting behind shields.

The Vikings left behind a rich legacy. This included language, styles of art and design, storytelling, boatbuilding, exploration, assemblies and parliaments. A thousand years later, everyone still wants to know about the Vikings' battles, adventures and ways of living.

3-second sum-up

The Viking age came to an end as powerful Christian kingdoms emerged in Europe. New ways of fighting were developed by the Normans.

3-minute mission Viking names

Today, there are still people whose surnames are based on the Viking system. Vikings identified babies as 'son of' or 'daughter of' their father. This is how it worked:

Eirik (= ever-powerful) **Thorvaldsson** (= son of Thorvald) **'the Red'** or **Sigrid** (= beautiful victory) **Tostadottir** (= daughter of Tosti) **'the Proud'**.

Vikings loved giving people nickames, too – often funny or rude ones! Try giving yourself one, such as James son-of-Tom 'the Nerd', or Lily daughter-of-Steve 'the Blue Haired'.

The Vikings' way of life still has an influence on our modern lives.

Traditional Viking styles of boatbuilding are still used to make a type of rowing boat called a skiff.

Up Helly Aa is a festival held in Shetland, introduced in the 1800s to celebrate Viking traditions by burning a Viking-style ship and carrying torches in a procession.

Many of the days of the week are based on Viking and Saxon names.

Sun   Mon   Tues   Wed   Thur   Fri   Sat

Some modern parliamentary traditions can be traced back to the Viking assemblies.

Icelandic assembly building called the Alpingishús.

Discover more

FICTION BOOKS

The Shield Ring
by Rosemary Sutcliff
Penguin, 1992

*The Viking Sagas 1 Bracelet
of Bones 2 Scramasax*
by Kevin Crossley-Holland
Quercus Children's Books, 2012

Thor and the Master of Magic
by Kevin Crossley-Holland
Barrington Stoke, 2013

MYTHS AND LEGENDS

Illustrated North Myths
by Alex Frith and Louie Stowell
Usborne, 2013

Norse Myths and Legends
by Anita Ganeri
Raintree, 2013

NON-FICTION BOOKS

100 Facts: Vikings
by Fiona Macdonald
Miles Kelly Publishing, 2008

Eyewitness: Viking
by Susan M Margeson
Dorling Kindersley, 2011

Greatest Warriors: Vikings
by Philip Steele
Arcturus Publishing 2013–2014

The Vicious Vikings by Terry Deary
Scholastic, 1998

ACTIVITY BOOKS

Hands on History: Vikings – Dress, Eat, Write and Play – just like the Vikings
by Fiona Macdonald
QED, 2011

Sigurd the Dragonslayer
by Dr. Ragnhild Ljosland
The Orcadian, 2014

WEBSITES

BBC resources
http://www.bbc.co.uk/history/ancient/vikings/

http://www.bbc.co.uk/education/topics/ztyr9j6

https://www.youtube.com/watch?v=taVsvYWp1UU

Information from Viking centres
http://jorvik-viking-centre.co.uk/who-were-the-vikings/

http://www.ribevikingecenter.dk/en/home.aspx

Viking game, National Museum of Scotland
http://www.nms.ac.uk/explore/games/vikings-training-school/

General reference
http://www.hurstwic.org/history/text/history.htm

To hear an Icelander pronounce hnefatafl
http://forvo.com/word/hnefatafl/

Although every endeavour has been made by the publisher to ensure that all content from these websites is educational material of the highest quality and is age appropriate, we strongly advise that Internet access is supervised by a responsible adult.

Index

Answers

Page 14: Crack the code!
THIS FISH IS A SHARK
THAT IS ITS FIN

Page 72: Days of the week
Tiw	Tyr	Tuesday
Woden	Odin	Wednesday
Thunre	Thor	Thursday
Frige	Frigg	Friday

Page 54: What's it for?
1. Sickle – Cutting corn
2. Shears – Cutting sheep's coats
3. Quern – Grinding grains